SOUS VIDE COOKBOOK

----- ❧❦❧ -----

Step By Step Guide And Proven Recipes For Sous Vide Meals

John Carter

© Copyright 2018 by John Carter - All rights reserved.

This document is geared towards providing exact and reliable information in regards to the topic and issue covered. The publication is sold with the idea that the publisher is not required to render accounting, officially permitted, or otherwise, qualified services. If advice is necessary, legal or professional, a practiced individual in the profession should be ordered.

- From a Declaration of Principles which was accepted and approved equally by a Committee of the American Bar Association and a Committee of Publishers and Associations.

In no way is it legal to reproduce, duplicate, or transmit any part of this document in either electronic means or in printed format. Recording of this publication is strictly prohibited and any storage of this document is not allowed unless with written permission from the publisher. All rights reserved.

The information provided herein is stated to be truthful and consistent, in that any liability, in terms of inattention or otherwise, by any usage or abuse of any policies, processes, or directions contained within is the solitary and utter responsibility of the recipient reader. Under no circumstances will any legal responsibility or blame be held against the publisher for any reparation, damages, or monetary loss due to the information herein, either directly or indirectly.

Respective authors own all copyrights not held by the publisher.

The information herein is offered for informational purposes solely, and is universal as so. The presentation of the information is without contract or any type of guarantee assurance.

The trademarks that are used are without any consent, and the publication of the trademark is without permission or backing by the trademark owner. All trademarks and brands within this book are for clarifying purposes only and are the owned by the owners themselves, not affiliated with this document.

Table of Contents

INTRODUCTION 1

CHAPTER ONE WHAT IS SOUS VIDE COOKING? 3

CHAPTER TWO SOUS VIDE HONEY-ROSEMARY LAMB SHANK 11

CHAPTER THREE SOUS VIDE BEER-BRAISED PORK SHANK 15

CHAPTER FOUR SOUS VIDE LAMB STEW 19

CHAPTER FIVE SOUS VIDE LEMON AND BLUEBERRY .. 21

CHAPTER SIX SOUS VIDE CHICKEN 23

CHAPTER SEVEN 72 HOURS SOUS VIDE BBQ SHORT RIBS 27

CHAPTER EIGHT TAIWANESE CORN ON THE COB 29

CHAPTER NINE SOUS VIDE CHUCK-EYE STEAK DIANE 31

CHAPTER TEN OVERNIGHT OATMEAL WITH STEWED FRUIT COMPOTE 35

CHAPTER ELEVEN ORANGE ROSEMARY INFUSED VINEGAR 37

CHAPTER TWELVE BLACKBERRY BASIL INFUSED VINEGAR 39

CHAPTER THIRTEEN CARROT AND DAIKON QUICK PICKLE 41

CHAPTER FOURTEEN CHOCOLATE ZABAGLIONE 43

CHAPTER FIFTEEN VANILLA BEAN ICE CREAM 45

CHAPTER SIXTEEN SOUS VIDE CORNED BEEF AND CABBAGE 47

CHAPTER SEVENTEEN SOUS VIDE BROWN BUTTER SCALLOPS 49

CHAPTER EIGHTEEN SOUS-VIDE CHAR SIU 51

CHAPTER NINETEEN SOUS VIDE SESAME SALMON WITH SOBA NOODLES 55

CHAPTER TWENTY PORK TENDERLOIN WITH ROSEMARY GARLIC MAPLE GLAZE 59

CHAPTER TWENTY ONE SOUS VIDE CHEESECAKE 61

CHAPTER TWENTY TWO SOUS VIDE BONELESS PORK CHOP 63

CHAPTER TWENTY THREE SOUS VIDE SHORT RIBS 65

CHAPTER TWENTY FOUR SOUS VIDE SAUSAGE 67

CHAPTER TWENTY FIVE SOUS VIDE HALIBUT 69

CHAPTER TWENTY SIX SOUS VIDE POACHED EGGS + AVOCADO TOAST 71

CHAPTER TWENTY SEVEN SOUS VIDE COD 73

CHAPTER TWENTY EIGHT SOUS VIDE COLD BREW COFFEE 75

CHAPTER TWENTY NINE SOUS VIDE GARLIC HERB BUTTER STEAK 77

CHAPTER THIRTY SOUS VIDE CARROTS 79

CHAPTER THIRTY ONE SOUS VIDE LAMB CHOPS WITH BASIL CHIMICHURRI 81

CHAPTER THIRTY TWO SOUS VIDE DUCK LEGS 83

CHAPTER THIRTY THREE SOUS VIDE SPICED AUBERGINE WITH TURMERIC AND COCONUT SAUCE, CASHEW BUTTER AND CRISPY KALE 85

CHAPTER THIRTY FOUR SOUS VIDE BRUSSELS SPROUTS AND SPROUT TOPS, MISO BUTTER, CASHEW 89

CHAPTER THIRTY FIVE SOUS VIDE LEEKS 91

CHAPTER THIRTY SIX POLENTA SOUS VIDE 93

CHAPTER THIRTY SEVEN SOUS VIDE FENNEL AND ORANGE QUINOA SALAD 95

CHAPTER THIRTY EIGHT BEETROOT WITH PICKLED QUINCE 99

CHAPTER THIRTY NINE SOUS VIDE POTATO RÖSTI ... 103

CHAPTER FORTY PUMPKIN VELOUTÉ WITH WILD MUSHROOMS 105

CHAPTER FORTY ONE PICKLED RADISH, DILL EMULSION AND PUFFED QUINOA 107

CHAPTER FORTY TWO SOUS VIDE PIGS EARS 111

CHAPTER FORTY THREE SUCKLING PIG WITH CHOU FARCI, HUMMUS AND CHICKPEA FRICASSEE 113

CHAPTER FORTY FOUR SOUS VIDE PORK BELLY 121

CHAPTER FORTY FIVE PORK SHOULDER WITH HISPI CABBAGE AND APPLES 123

CHAPTER FORTY SIX TEQUILA CHICKEN 129

CHAPTER FORTY SEVEN SOUS VIDE CHICKEN WITH ENGLISH MUSTARD AND BROAD BEANS 131

CHAPTER FORTY EIGHT SOUS VIDE MACKEREL 135

CHAPTER FORTY NINE SOUS VIDE SEA BASS 137

CHAPTER FIFTY SOUS VIDE BEEF AND PRUNE TAGINE 139

CHAPTER FIFTY ONE SPICED PINEAPPLE WITH WHIPPED CREAM CHEESE YOGHURT AND GINGER BISCUITS 143

INTRODUCTION

So you are all ready to try sous vide for yourself, but are at a loss of where to start? Or you have already begun your sous vide exploration and are ready to elevate your recipes to the next level?

Either way, we've got the cookbook for you. Sous vide is a fairly simple method of cooking that employs submersion of sealed bags of food in water that is held at a specific temperature for a precise amount of time. This is done to cook the food perfectly at the desired level of doneness. You can cook the same thing over and over again with the same delicious results knowing it will be good each time.

Getting started with sous vide cooking can be a bit daunting for those without experience, even though this revolutionary method of cooking is easy to learn. It's important for beginners to read up on the sous vide process in order to obtain the best performance from your device and to ensure safety. On the other hand, even those who are experienced with sous vide can learn incredible tips and new mouthwatering recipes to add to their own sous vide cooking arsenal. While I do encourage sous vide enthusiasts to research information online, having a sous vide cookbook in your kitchen is an absolute must – especially for the quick and easy sous vide time and temperature chart.

CHAPTER ONE
WHAT IS SOUS VIDE COOKING?

Once limited to the pros, sous vide (pronounced sue-veed) is a cooking method that uses specific temperature control to deliver consistent, restaurant-quality results. High-end restaurants have been making use of sous vide cooking for ages to prepare food to the exact level of doneness desired, every time. The method recently became famous for home cooks with the availability of reasonably priced and easy-to-use sous vide precision cooking equipments.

Sous vide, which means "under vacuum" in French, is the process of vacuum-sealing food in a bag, then cooking it to a very precise temperature inside a water bath. This method produces results that are cannot be achieved through any other method of cooking.

Sous vide cooking is a lot easier than you might think, and typically involves three simple steps:

1. Affix your precision cooker to a pot of water and set the time and temperature according to the level of doneness you desire.

2. Put your food inside a sealable bag and clip it to the side of the pot.

3. Finish up by searing, grilling, or broiling the food to put in a crispy, golden exterior layer.

SOUS VIDE COOKBOOK

Why should I cook sous vide?

Sous vide cooking makes use of precise temperature control with circulation to produce results that you can't achieve with any other cooking method. The reason is when using the conventional methods of cooking, you don't have power over heat and temperature. As a result, it's very hard and time consuming to consistently cook good food. Food ends up overcooked on the outside, with only a small portion in the center that is cooked to the temperature you desire. Food loses its flavor, overcooks easily, and ends up with a dry, chewy texture.

With precise temperature control in the kitchen, sous vide gives the following benefits:

Consistency

Since you cook your food to a specific temperature for a precise amount of time, you can look forward to very consistent results.

Taste

Food cooks in its juices. This makes sure that the food is moist, juicy and tender.

Waste reduction

Traditionally prepared food dries out and leads to waste. For instance, on average, conventionally cooked steak loses up to 40% of its volume due to drying out. Steak cooked through precision cooking, loses none of its volume.

Flexibility

Traditional cooking can necessitate your regular attention. Precision cooking brings food to an precise temperature and holds it. There is no need to be anxious about overcooking.

How are sous vide results better?

Sous vide supplies down-to-the-degree control in the kitchen to deliver the most tender, flavorful food you've ever had. With this, it is super simple to get restaurant-quality results from edge to edge.

What equipment do I need to cook sous vide?

It's actually very cheap and easy to get started with sous vide cooking thanks to the recent availability of sous vide equipments created for the home cook. You'll need a few things:

- A sous vide precision cooking device
- Packaging for your food, like resealable bags or canning jars
- A container to hold the water

Types of Sous Vide Machines

Sous vide equipment has been in existence for decades in professional kitchens all over the world, but it has always been huge, expensive, and overloaded with multifaceted features. This type of equipment finally made its way into high-end specialty retail shops, but remained restricted to chefs and consumers with broad culinary experience.

SOUS VIDE COOKBOOK

Cooking shows, social media, and online communities have furthered consumers' knowledge of sous vide cooking, and now sous vide has become accessible to home cooks. There are now lots of sous vide options available to the home cook.

Below are a few types of devices for you to consider when you're ready to create your ultimate sous vide setup:

Sous Vide Immersion Circulator

The Immersion circulator heats water and circulates it around the pot to maintain precise temperatures evenly. Immersion circulators are a cheap and an easy-to-use sous vide machine option. They do not come with a built-in water bath, so they take up very little space in your kitchen. The immersion circulator sous vide devices don't need additional equipment to get started because they clamp on and alter to any pot you already have.

Sous Vide Water Oven

Water ovens are usually referred to as countertop water baths. They are fully-contained, sous vide devices that are about the size of a microwave and normally cost $500+. Sous vide water ovens heat water, but unlike immersion circulators, they do not circulate the water. This can lead to irregularity in the food's resulting texture. Examples of water ovens include SousVide Supreme, AquaChef, and Gourmia. Multi-use cookers like Oliso, Gourmia and Instant Pot also offer sous vide appliances.

DIY Sous Vide Hacks

Cooler, rice cooker, and slow cooker hacks are good options for exploring sous vide cooking before you decide to buy a device. The Food Lab's J. Kenji Lopez-Alt has a great post on sous vide beer cooler hacks.

Sous Vide Packaging

Sealing foods prevents evaporation and allows for the most efficient transfer energy from the water to the food. To do so, simply place your seasoned food in a plastic bag and release the air using the water immersion method, a straw, or a vacuum sealer.

You don't need a vacuum sealer to cook sous vide. There are lots of options, here are a few of the best types of sous vide packaging:

Sous Vide Containers

Containers clip onto the side of any pot or vessel with an adjustable clamp. So, you can use any size of pot that you already have at home. If you're planning to cook a lot of food at once, plastic bins like Cambro and Rubbermaid are great choices.

You can also explore creating a dedicated sous vide cooking vessel.

Resealable Bags or Jars

Resealable bags are very resourceful, and can be used with the water immersion method to eliminate air from the bag. We suggest heavy-duty, BPA-free bags, like Ziplock's freezer bags.

Reusable Silicone Bags

Reusable sous vide bags made from silicone, like these Stasher Reusable Silicone Sous Vide Bag bags; make it easy to enjoy the same quality results night after night.

Vacuum Sealing Bags

You don't need to buy a vacuum sealer and vacuum seal bags, but they work great for batch cooking. Foodsaver and Oliso are good options, and both are pretty inexpensive.

Canning Jars

Numerous different types of foods can also be cooked in glass canning jars. Beans and grains both cook well in jars, as do desserts such as cakes and custards.

How do I get set up for my first sous vide cook?

Getting set up with your first sous vide cook is easy:

1. Simply clip the Sous Vide Precision Cooker to a pot or container and fill with water above the minimum fill line.

2. Season your food and put it in the bag. Put the bag in the water bath and clip it to the side of the pot.

3. Choose what you're cooking from our compilation of recipes and sous vide guides, then press start on the screen of your cooker.

CHAPTER TWO
SOUS VIDE HONEY-ROSEMARY LAMB SHANK

We love lamb in all its gamey glory, but not everybody feels the same way. Nevertheless, with this big flavorful recipe for honey-rosemary lamb shank, we've been able to change a few lamb-fearing hearts and minds.

After 48 hours with Sous Vide Precision Cooker, the meat is fall-off-the-bone soft and the vegetables deeply seasoned. A fast reduction of the cooking liquid finishes the vegetables to perfection and makes a rich, aromatic, and perfectly sweet sauce that balances the often-bold taste of lamb.

Ingredients for 4

- 4 lamb shanks
- 2 tablespoons olive oil
- 2 cups all-purpose flour for dusting
- 1 medium yellow onion, peeled and thinly sliced
- 4 garlic cloves, peeled and smashed
- 4 medium carrots, medium dice
- 4 stalks celery, medium dice
- 3 tablespoons tomato paste
- 1/2 cup sherry wine vinegar

- 1 cup red wine
- 3/4 cup honey
- 1 quart beef stock
- 4 sprigs fresh rosemary
- 2 dried bay leaves
- Kosher salt and freshly ground black pepper

How to prepare

- Set your Sous Vide Precision Cooker to 155°F (68.3°C).
- In a big cast-iron skillet, heat oil over high heat until just starting to smoke. Season shanks richly with salt, dust with flour, and sear to golden brown on all sides.
- Take out shanks and set aside. Reduce heat to medium-high and add onion, garlic, carrots, and celery. Season with salt and pepper and cook for 10 minutes. Add in tomato paste and cook for one minute.
- Add in vinegar, wine, honey, stock, rosemary, and bay leaves and cook for two minutes.
- Add in vegetables, sauce, and lamb shanks to vacuum or Ziploc plastic bag, seal, and cook for 48 hours.
- Take out shanks from bag and pat dry, reserving cooking liquid. Place shanks on roasting rack and broil until skin is golden brown, about five minutes. (Watch carefully to make sure it doesn't burn.)

- Add in cooking liquid and vegetables to large saucepan and simmer over medium-high heat until vegetables are tender and sauce is minimized by two-thirds, about 10 minutes.

- Remove shanks from oven, sauce, and serve. For smaller portions, pull the meat from the shank in large chunks and serve with sauce.

CHAPTER THREE
SOUS VIDE BEER-BRAISED PORK SHANK

Ingredients for 4

- 4 pork shanks
- 2 tablespoons extra-virgin olive oil
- 2 cups all-purpose flour for dusting
- 1 medium yellow onion, peeled and thinly sliced
- 4 garlic cloves, peeled and smashed
- 4 medium carrots, medium dice
- 4 stalks celery, medium dice
- 2 tablespoons tomato paste
- 24 ounces of your favorite full-flavored beer (e.g. porter, stout, ale)
- 2 tablespoons soy sauce
- 2 tablespoons honey
- 1 quart pork stock (or chicken or beef)
- 4 sprigs fresh thyme
- 4 sprigs fresh rosemary

- 2 bay leaves
- Kosher salt and freshly ground black pepper

How to prepare

- Set Anova Sous Vide Precision Cooker to 155°F (68.3°C).
- In a large cast-iron skillet, heat oil over high heat until just starting to smoke. Season shanks richly with salt, dust with flour, and sear to golden brown on all sides.
- Take out shanks and set aside. Minimize heat to medium-high and add onion, garlic, carrots, and celery. Season with salt and pepper and cook for 10 minutes. Add tomato paste and cook for one minute.
- Add in beer, soy sauce, honey, stock, thyme, rosemary, and bay leaves and cook for two minutes.
- Add in vegetables, sauce, and pork shanks to vacuum or Ziploc plastic bag, seal, and cook for 48 hours.
- Remove shanks from bag and pat dry, reserving cooking liquid. Place shanks on roasting rack and broil until skin is golden brown, about five minutes. (Watch carefully to make sure they don't burn.)
- Add in cooking liquid and vegetables to large saucepan and simmer over medium-high heat until vegetables are tender and sauce reduced by two-thirds, about 10 minutes.

- Remove shanks from oven, sauce, and serve. For smaller portions, pull the meat from the shank in large chunks and serve with sauce.

CHAPTER FOUR
SOUS VIDE LAMB STEW

Ingredients for 6

- 2 pounds boneless lamb shoulder, cut into 1-inch cubes
- 4 ounces thick-cut bacon, cut into ½ strips
- 1 cup red wine
- 2 tablespoons tomato paste
- 1 quart beef stock
- 4 large shallots, quartered
- 4 medium carrots, peeled and cut into 1-inch pieces
- 4 stalks of celery, cut into 1-inch pieces
- 3 garlic cloves, peeled and smashed
- 1 pound small fingerling potatoes (or small red), cut in half lengthwise
- 4 ounces dried shiitake mushrooms (optional)
- 3 sprigs fresh rosemary
- 3 sprigs fresh thyme
- 2 dried whole bay leaves
- Kosher salt and freshly ground black pepper

How to prepare

- Set the Sous Vide Precision Cooker to 145°F (62.7°C).

- Heat a big cast-iron skillet over medium-high heat. Render bacon until it is golden brown and set aside.

- Season the lamb evenly with salt and pepper and sear in bacon fat until it is golden brown on all sides. (You will likely have to work in several batches.)

- Set lamb to another side and deglaze pan with wine and stock. Add in wine-stock combination, bacon, lamb, any accumulated searing juices, vegetables, and herbs to a large Ziplock or vacuum bag. Seal the bag and cook it for 24 hours.

- Pour the contents of the bag into a big saucepan, removing the pieces of lamb to a plate. (This makes sure the meat doesn't get overcooked or tough while the sauce and vegetables simmer.) Simmer over medium heat until the vegetables are tender and the sauce reduced by half, about 15 minutes.

- Remove the saucepan from the heat, take out the lamb to the pan to warm in the sauce, and serve.

CHAPTER FIVE
SOUS VIDE LEMON AND BLUEBERRY

Crème brûlée is a crowd-pleasing standard French dessert. It can be prepared without stress ahead of time and stored in the refrigerator then quickly finished at the dinner table, making it a great option for a dinner party dessert.

Ingredients for 6

- 6 large egg yolks
- 1 1/3 cups superfine sugar, plus more for sprinkling
- 3 cups heavy (whipping) cream
- Zest of 2 lemons
- 4 tablespoons freshly squeezed lemon juice
- 1 teaspoon vanilla extract
- 1 cup fresh blueberries

How to prepare

- Set your Sous Vide Precision Cooker to 195°F (90.5°C).
- With an electric mixer, whisk together the egg yolks and sugar in a large bowl until it is pale and creamy. Set it aside.
- Pour the cream into a medium saucepan over medium heat and heat to just below boiling point. Be cautious

not to burn the cream. Add in the lemon zest, lemon juice, and vanilla into the cream, stirring as you add the lemon juice to evade curdling. Simmer over low heat for 4 to 5 minutes.

- Take out the cream mixture from the heat and cool for 2 to 3 minutes. When cooled, pour a small amount into the egg mixture and whisk to combine. (This tempers the egg mixture so it doesn't scramble when you pour in the rest of the hot cream concoction.) Pour the remaining of the cream mixture into the eggs and stir to mix.

- Divide the blueberries equally among six mini mason jars then pour the egg-cream mixture over the blueberries, dividing equally among the jars.

- Screw on the jar lids to fingertip tightness and position in the water bath, ensuring they are completely underwater. Cook for 45 minutes.

- Take out the jars from the water bath and place in the refrigerator for at least 5 hours or up to 4 days.

- To serve, remove the lids and sprinkle a thin layer of sugar over the top of the crème brûlée. Caramelize the sugar using a blowtorch.

CHAPTER SIX
SOUS VIDE CHICKEN

The secret here is briefly searing the chicken in a cast-iron skillet before serving.

Ingredients

- Chicken thighs
- Salt

How to prepare

- Clip the circulator onto the side of a large stockpot and fill it with water until it reaches between the Min and Max line. Tap the screen to turn it on then rotate the green dial until the number on the bottom reads 150.0 F. The number on top is the present temperature. Allow to preheat.

- Wash and carefully dry boneless, skin-on chicken thighs. If you can only find thighs with the bone-in. Season both sides with salt and pepper. On the skinless side, place a few sprigs of your favorite herbs (here we used thyme and rosemary) along with a small pad of butter.

- Place one chicken thigh into a quart-sized (or larger) high-quality zip-top bag. We like to roll back the top so the zipper doesn't get chicken-y. Repeat for the rest of the thighs. If you're using a larger bag, you can put more than one thigh, as long as they are side-by-side and not on top of each other.

- Now we have to get all of the air out of the bags and seal them up. Fill another pot with cold water and, with the top of the bag still open, submerge the bottom of the bag into the water. This is known as the water displacement method. Keep pushing the bag into the water, allowing the water to press the air out.

- Drop all of the bags into the preheated pot and let them go for 1.5 hours. Remember, even if you forget about it for another 30 minutes (or longer), the chicken literally cannot overcook. Make sure that all the bags are submerged under water. If they aren't, just repeat the water displacement method above to ensure all the air is out.

- Just like blanching vegetables, remove the bags from the water and dunk them into a bowl filled with ice water. Chill for 10-15 minutes until cooled.

- This step is optional, but we like the results when you do it. Place the bags of chicken, skin side down, on a baking sheet. Place another baking sheet on top, weigh down with a cast iron pan or heavy cans, and allow it to sit for 30 minutes. This helps get a flatter skin that will crisp up beautifully. If you're going to eat the chicken later in the week, just transfer the bags to the fridge after this step.

- When you're ready to eat, remove the chicken from the bag and dry it very well. It may not look the most attractive now, but just wait.

- Preheat a pan (we prefer cast iron) over medium high heat, add a few tablespoons of oil, and sear the chicken skin-side down for 2-3 minutes until It is golden and crispy. Turn and cook for another 2-3 minutes. Slice, sprinkle with a touch of salt, and serve with roasted potatoes, and asparagus.

CHAPTER SEVEN
72 HOURS SOUS VIDE BBQ SHORT RIBS

Ingredients

- 3/4 cup unsweetened pineapple juice
- 1/2 cup peanut oil
- 1/3 cup soy sauce
- 1/4 cup molasses
- 1 teaspoon ground ginger
- 1 lbs short ribs
- 1 teaspoon (or more) Kosher salt and freshly ground black pepper to taste

How to prepare

BBQ Sauce

- Mix the first five ingredients, mixing well
- In a glass bowl, cover up the short ribs with the sauce. Cover and refrigerate overnight.

For sous vide

- Preheat sous vide to 54 °C / 131 °F.

- Vacuum seal the ribs, with sauce. Place into water bath and cook for 72-hours.

For slow cooker

- Add ribs with sauce to your slow cooker. Cook on LOW for 9 hours. Do not cook on high--this must be done low and slow to prevent toughness.

CHAPTER EIGHT
TAIWANESE CORN ON THE COB

Spicy, garlicky roast corn is a much loved Taiwanese street food snack--here's a quick, 20 minute version of that dish.

Ingredients

- 3 ears of summer corn
- 3 cloves garlic
- 3 Tbsp dark soy sauce
- 2 Tbsp chili sauce
- 1 Tbsp sugar
- 1 stalk green onion, rough chop
- 2 Tbsp butter
- Finishing salt

How to prepare

- Set your water bath to 85°C (185°F)
- Pour in garlic, soy sauce, chili sauce, sugar, green onions, and butter in a food processor and puree until it is smooth.
- Pour in mixture into a bag with corn and vacuum-seal. If you don't have a vacuum sealer, you can make use of

a freezer-safe zip bag and seal with the water displacement method. You might need to use a weight or a wedge to keep the bag submerged underwater. Sous vide for 20 minutes.

- After 20 minutes, take out the corn from water bath. You can give the corn a nice char on the grill, broil on high for a couple minutes, or use a blow torch.

CHAPTER NINE
SOUS VIDE CHUCK-EYE STEAK DIANE

Steak Diane is rich, standard, and totally delicious — not to mention you get to play with fire.

Ingredients for 4

- 4 6-8-ounce beef chuck-eye steaks
- 1 tablespoon extra virgin olive oil
- 4 tablespoons butter
- 4 sprigs fresh thyme
- 2 tablespoons minced shallot
- 8 ounces crimini mushrooms, thinly sliced
- ¼ cup Cognac (or any decent brandy)
- 1 tablespoon Dijon mustard
- 2 teaspoons Worcestershire sauce
- 1 cup beef stock
- ½ cup heavy cream
- Kosher salt and freshly ground black pepper
- Minced fresh chives for garnish

SOUS VIDE COOKBOOK

How to prepare

- Set your Sous Vide Precision Cooker to 132°F (55.5°C).

- Season steaks generously with kosher salt.

- Seal steaks in a vacuum or Ziploc plastic bag and cook for six hours.

- Remove the steaks, reserving the cooking liquid, and pat dry.

- In a large cast-iron skillet, heat olive oil and two tablespoons of the butter over medium-high, until just beginning to smoke. Add fresh thyme and steaks and sear on both sides until dark golden brown, basting with butter and thyme as you cook. Remove steaks from the pan and set aside.

- Discard butter, oil, and thyme and add two tablespoons of fresh butter to the pan over medium heat. Add shallots and mushrooms and saute until tender, about five minutes.

- Deglaze pan with Cognac (stand back if you want to keep your eyebrows) and add mustard, Worcestershire, beef stock, and reserved cooking liquid from the bag, as well as whatever has accumulated on plate holding cooked steaks.

- Simmer sauce until reduced by half, about five minutes. Add cream and season as needed with Kosher salt and freshly ground black pepper and cook for two more minutes. (The sous vide cooking liquid will have a decent amount of salt from the steak seasoning, so taste first before adding additional salt.)

- To finish, remove pan from the heat and add steaks to the sauce, coating both sides and letting sit for about a minute to bring them back to temperature.

- Alternatively, you can slice the steaks individually and top immediately with the warm sauce. Garnish with minced chives.

CHAPTER TEN
OVERNIGHT OATMEAL WITH STEWED FRUIT COMPOTE

You can double the recipe in the same pouch for 4 servings but for more than 4 servings, make use of additional pouches

Ingredients

For the oatmeal

- 1 cup (90g) rolled oats
- 3 cups (710 ml) water
- 1 pinch salt
- 1 pinch cinnamon

For the stewed fruit compote

- ¾ cup (100g) dried fruit (any mix of the following – cherries, blueberries, golden raisins, apricots, cranberries)
- 2 tablespoons(25g) white sugar
- ½ cup (118 ml) of water
- 2 drops of vanilla extract
- 1/2 lemon, for zest, finely grated
- 1/2 orange, for zest, finely grated

SOUS VIDE COOKBOOK

How to prepare

- Fill and preheat the Sous Vide water oven to 155F/68C.

- Place a large (gallon/3.8 liter) zip-closure cooking pouch in a baggy rack. (If you don't own a baggy rack, you can always ask somebody to hold the bag open while you put in the contents.)

- Pour the oatmeal, water, salt and cinnamon into the zip-closure cooking pouch, and use the displacement method to remove the air and zip the seal closed.

- Immerse the sealed pouch in the water bath.

- Put a (quart/0.95 liter) zip-closure cooking pouch in a baggy rack and pour in the dried fruit, sugar, and water, and vanilla, orange and lemon zest. Use the displacement method to remove the air and zip the seal closed.

- Immerse the pouch in the water bath with the oatmeal.

- Six to ten hours later, take out the pouches from the water bath. Give the oatmeal pouch a fast shake and pour straight into two bowls.

- Open the pouch with the stewed fruit, spoon the fruit compote on top of the oatmeal, serve and enjoy.

CHAPTER ELEVEN
ORANGE ROSEMARY INFUSED VINEGAR

Ingredients

- 10 blood oranges (or 5 navel oranges) for zest
- 10 fresh rosemary springs
- 4 cups (.9 liters) white balsamic vinegar

How to prepare

- Fill and preheat the SousVide cooker to 153F/67C.
- Zest the oranges, being cautious to use only the orange surface of the peel, and not the white inner layer.
- In a big (gallon 3.8 liter) zip-closure cooking pouch, mix the zest with the rosemary and vinegar, evacuate the air, and zip the pouch closed.
- Submerge in the water oven and cook for 2 to 3 hours.
- Strain the vinegar through cheesecloth or a fine mesh strainer, pour into a clean bottle, and seal.

CHAPTER TWELVE
BLACKBERRY BASIL INFUSED VINEGAR

Ingredients

- 3 cups (12 oz/340 g) of blackberries
- 1/2 cup (1.3 oz/34 g) basil leaves
- 4 cups (16 fl oz/473 ml) white balsamic vinegar

How to prepare

- Fill and preheat the SousVide cooker to 153°F/ 67°C.
- Combine ingredients in a large (1 gallon/3.8 liter) zip-closure cooking pouch, evacuate the air, and zip closed.
- Immerse in the water bath and cook for 2 to 3 hours.
- Partway via the cooking process, squeeze the pouch to tenderize the blackberries.
- Strain the vinegar through cheesecloth or a fine mesh strainer and get rid of the solids.
- Pour the infusion into a clean bottle; cap tightly, label, date, and store in the refrigerator for up to six weeks.

CHAPTER THIRTEEN
CARROT AND DAIKON QUICK PICKLE

Ingredients

- 2 teaspoons (10 ml) kosher salt
- 1/4 cup (48 g) sugar
- 1/2 cup plus 2 tablespoons (135 ml) white vinegar
- 1/2 cup (120 ml) warm water
- 1/2 pound carrots (228 g) peeled and cut into matchsticks
- 1 1/2 pounds daikon (228 g) peeled and cut into matchsticks

How to prepare

- Fill and preheat the SousVide cooker to 140F/60C.
- Pour the carrots and daikon into a small (quart/0.9 liter) zip-closure cooking pouch (or chamber vacuum pouch.)
- In a bowl, whisk together the salt, sugar, vinegar, and water and pour the concoction over the vegetables.
- Remove the air from the zip-closure pouch and zip the seal (or vacuum seal in the chamber vacuum.)

- Immerse the pouch in the water oven to cook for 15 minutes.

- Take out the pouch from the water oven and quick chill, immerse in an ice water bath for 15 minutes.

- Refrigerate for use within 4 weeks.

CHAPTER FOURTEEN
CHOCOLATE ZABAGLIONE

Ingredients

- 8 large egg yolks
- 1 cup (192 g) sugar
- Pinch salt
- 1/2 cup (120 ml) dry Marsala
- 1/3 cup (37 g) unsweetened cocoa powder
- 1/4 cup (60 ml) whipping cream, or heavy cream
- 1 pound (0.45 kg) fresh strawberries, washed, hulled, and quartered

How to prepare

- Fill and preheat the SousVide cooker to 165F/74C.
- In the meantime, in a bowl, whisk together the egg yolks, sugar, salt and Marsala.
- Add in cocoa powder and whisk until it is totally combined, then add cream and whisk well.
- Pour the egg mixture into a large (gallon/3.8 liter) zip-closure cooking pouch.
- Remove the air from the pouch and zip the seal.

- Immerse the pouch in the water oven to cook for 20 to 30 minutes until it is thick and creamy. Occasionally, lift the pouch from the water bath and massage the contents through the pouch to mix and return to the water.

- Meanwhile, divide the strawberries among individual dessert bowls or stemmed cocktail glasses.

- When ready to serve, pour the warm zabaglione over the strawberries, or if you desire, pour the zabaglione into individual serving bowls, cover, and chill until set in the refrigerator, then garnish each bowl with a few fresh strawberries at serving.

CHAPTER FIFTEEN
VANILLA BEAN ICE CREAM

Ingredients

- 6 large egg yolks
- 1 cup (75 g) superfine (castor) sugar
- 1/4 cup (29 g) non-fat dry milk powder (organic if available)
- 1 quart (.9 liter) half-and-half
- 1/2 vanilla bean

How to prepare

- Fill and preheat the water oven to 140F/60C.
- In a bowl, beat the egg yolks with the sugar and non-fat dry milk until it is light yellow and thickened.
- Scrape the seeds from the vanilla bean and add them and the half and half to the yolks and beat just enough to mix.
- Pour the concoction into a large (gallon/3.8 liter) zip-closure cooking pouch; remove the air from the pouch and zip it closed. (If you are using standard vacuum seal pouches, press out as much air as possible from the pouch with your hands and seal only. Do not attempt to seal liquids using a suction vacuum sealer.)

- Immerse the pouch in the water oven and cook for 45 minutes to 1 hour.

- Remove the pouch from the water bath and quick chill it, immersed in ice water (half ice/half water) for 30 minutes. Refrigerate until ready to churn.

- Churn the chilled mixture according to your ice cream machine's manufacturer's instructions.

- Serve immediately, or if you want, scoop into a quart container, cover it tightly, and freeze for one hour before serving if you desire a firmer consistency.

CHAPTER SIXTEEN
SOUS VIDE CORNED BEEF AND CABBAGE

Ingredients

- 4 pounds (1.81 kg) of corned beef
- 6 slices of bacon, cut into ½ inch (1.3 cm) strips
- 1 head of cabbage, cut into 1-inch (3 cm) strips
- 2 cups (470 ml) chicken stock
- 1/2 cup (120 ml) champagne vinegar

How to prepare

- Pre-heat the water oven to 134°F/56°C.
- Put the corned beef into a cooking pouch and vacuum/seal.
- Immerse the pouch in the water oven and cook for 48 hours
- About 45 minutes before you are ready to serve the meal, prepare the cabbage.
- In a skillet, over medium heat, cook the bacon pieces until they are crisp and the fat is rendered. Pour off all but 1-2 tablespoons (15 to 30 ml) of the bacon fat.

- Add in the cabbage strips to the skillet, raise the heat to medium-high, and cook for about 5 minutes.

- Add the chicken stock and the vinegar to the pan and continue to cook the cabbage in the liquid until tender.

- When the cabbage is almost tender, remove the corned beef from the water bath and the cooking pouch.

- To serve, slice the corned beef into 1/2" – 3/4" (1.3 cm – 2 cm) slices and serve over the cabbage.

CHAPTER SEVENTEEN
SOUS VIDE BROWN BUTTER SCALLOPS

Ingredients

- 1 package SizzleFish Scallops (about 4.25oz)
- 2 tsp brown butter (1 tsp for cooking + 1 tsp for searing)*
- salt & pepper, as desired

How to prepare

- Fill up your pot with water
- Preheat the sous vide circulator to 140 degrees
- Pat your scallops dry with a paper towel
- Place scallops, 1 tsp brown butter, salt and pepper in a ziploc bag
- Seal tight, making sure to remove all air
- Put the bag in the water and ensure that it stays underwater
- Set timer for 35 minutes (They can take up to 40 minutes)
- Once done, take out from the water and bag

- Pat the scallops dry
- Heat up your left over tsp of brown butter in a pan over high heat
- Add your scallops to the pan to get a golden sear (about 30 seconds per side)
- Serve as desired

Notes

- Feel free to use any oil you choose

CHAPTER EIGHTEEN
SOUS-VIDE CHAR SIU

Ingredients

- 1kg Berkshire or Kurobuta pork neck
- Marinade
- 6 scallions, sliced into 2 inch lengths and smashed
- 8 garlic cloves, smashed and peeled
- 3 tablespoons regular soy sauce
- 2 tablespoons Chinese rice wine
- 3 tablespoons sugar
- 2.5 tablespoons hoisin sauce
- 2 tablespoons rich chicken stock
- 1 teaspoon sesame oil

How to prepare

- Mix all the marinade ingredients together well.
- Cut the pork lengthwise into strips around 2.5-3 inches wide and 2 inches or so thick. Cut strips diagonally, if needed, into pieces 6-8 inches long. Position it in a big baking dish that can accommodate all the pork in one layer. Pour the marinade atop the pork. Seal the dish

with cling wrap overnight, at least 12 hours and up to 36 hours. Turn the pork a few times during the marinating process. Keep in the fridge.

- Prepare a water bath, using an immersion circulator, and bring the water to 58 degrees Celsius

- Place each piece of pork, with some marinade, into a vacuum-sealable bag and seal at high pressure.

- Drop the bags into the water bath and cook for 24 hours. Once done, prepare an ice water bath and plunge the bags of pork directly into the ice water. Once cool, dry off the bags and either freeze or put in the fridge. Or open the bags, liberate your pork, and move to the final step of finishing off the pork.

Finishing Sauce (enough for two strips)

- 1 teaspoon salt

- 1 tablespoon hoisin sauce

- 2 teaspoons honey

How to prepare

- Mix the above together and taste. It should be salty-sweet.

- Preheat your oven to the highest temperature it can go. Pour some water into a roasting pan. Over the pan, place a large wire rack that fits over the top of the pan.

- Brush as much of the finishing sauce onto the strips of pork. You want it thick. Lay the pork on the wire rack (and over the water in the roasting pan). Pop this in the oven for 10 minutes or until the surface of the char siu is nicely charred.

- Alternatively, instead of using the oven, blowtorch the pork until charred.

CHAPTER NINETEEN
SOUS VIDE SESAME SALMON WITH SOBA NOODLES

Ingredients

For salmon:

- 2 (6-ounce) sashimi-grade salmon filets, with skin
- Salt and pepper
- 1 teaspoon sesame oil
- 1 cup extra virgin olive oil
- 1 tablespoon fresh ginger, grated
- 2 tablespoons honey

For sesame soba:

- 4 ounces dry soba noodles
- 1 tablespoon grape seed oil
- 2 cloves of garlic, chopped
- 1/2 head of broccoli
- 3 tablespoons tahini
- 1 teaspoon sesame oil

- 2 teaspoons extra virgin olive oil
- 1/4 lime, juiced
- 1 stalk green onion, sliced
- 1/4 cup cilantro, roughly chopped
- 1 teaspoon toasted sesame seeds
- Sesame seeds and lime wedges, for garnish

How to prepare

- Set up sous vide water bath, and set temperature of the sous vide to 51°C (123.8°F).
- In a medium-sized mixing bowl, mix up sesame oil, olive oil, ginger, and honey. In a quart-sized freezer-safe zip bag, add seasoned filets and seasoning mixture. Seal and sous vide at 51°C (123.8°F) for 20 minutes.
- While the fish is cooking, prepare soba noodles according to package directions.
- In the meantime, in a skillet over medium-high heat, heat grape seed oil. Stir-fry garlic and broccoli until soft, about 6-8 minutes.
- In a small mixing bowl, whisk together tahini, sesame oil, olive oil, lime juice, green onions, cilantro, and toasted sesame seeds. Mix into cooked and drained soba noodles, and toss in stir-fried broccoli and garlic.

- Heat a skillet over medium-high heat. Position a piece of parchment paper on the bottom of the skillet (the parchment paper will keep the skin from sticking to the pan). Turn up the heat to high, and transfer salmon to the pan, skin side down. Sear until skin is crisp, about 30 seconds to 1 minute.

- Divide soba noodles into two bowls; top with salmon, sesame seeds, and a lime wedge.

CHAPTER TWENTY
PORK TENDERLOIN WITH ROSEMARY GARLIC MAPLE GLAZE

The rosemary garlic maple rub is so delicious. It is highly recommended to make extra to glaze after cooking and add to your apple / onion hash.

Ingredients

- 1 1lb pork tenderloin
- ½ pink lady (or other tart) apple, cut into small cubes
- ½ large white or yellow onion, diced
- 1 tsp butter
- Rosemary Garlic Maple glaze
- 3 large sprigs rosemary
- 2 garlic cloves, mashed into a paste
- ¼ cup olive oil
- 1 tbsp maple syrup
- Large pinch salt

How to prepare

- Preheat sous vide machine to 135 degrees F.

- Mix all glaze ingredients in a food processor.

- Set aside nearly 1/3 of the mixture. Use the rest to rub all over pork loin. Add in some additional salt to the loin. Vacuum seal loin and place into the 135 F water bath. Cook for 2.5 hours.

- Take out pork from bag. Heat a nonstick skillet with butter until sizzling. Add in pork and sear, rotating, so all sides get a toasty brown, about 45-60 seconds / side. Take out pork and set aside.

- Using the same skillet, add your apples and onions and a tbsp of the reserved glaze.

- Slice pork, spooning any extra glaze on top. Serve with a rich scoop of apple and onion hash. Salt more to taste if necessary

CHAPTER TWENTY ONE
SOUS VIDE CHEESECAKE

Ingredients

- 16 oz Cream Cheese
- 3 Eggs
- ¾ Cup Sugar
- ½ tbs. Vanilla Extract
- ¼ Cup Sour Cream
- Fruit to top, if desired

Crust

- ½ Package of Graham Crackers (About 4-5), Crushed
- 1 tbs. Sugar
- 3 tbs. Unsalted Butter, Melted
- ¼ Tsp Cinnamon

How to prepare

- Preheat water bath to 176F.
- Crush graham crackers into very fine pieces. I place them in a sandwich bag and use a rolling pin.

- Add sugar, melted butter, and cinnamon. Mix thoroughly.

- Place crust mixture at the bottom of 8 4oz canning jars and firmly pack down.

- (Optional) Bake crust and jars for 10 minutes at 350F.

- Add room temperature cream cheese, eggs, sugar, sour cream, and vanilla into a large mixing bowl and mix thoroughly.

- Add cheesecake mixture to each canning jar, leaving about ½ inch from the top.

- Tighten canning jar lids using ONLY your fingertips, ensuring not to fully tighten as air must escape during the cooking process.

- Cook for 1 hour 30 minutes.

- Carefully remove from water bath using tongs and let chill on the counter until cool to touch (about 1 hour).

- Place cheesecakes in refrigerator for at least 4 hours.

- Open lid, top with fresh fruit or blueberry filling, and enjoy!

CHAPTER TWENTY TWO
SOUS VIDE BONELESS PORK CHOP

Pork is the unsung hero in the sous vide world. When it comes to sous vide boneless pork chops, the thicker the better.

Ingredients

- Thick cut boneless pork chops
- Salt and pepper
- (optional) Marinade of Choice

How to prepare

- (Optional) Marinate pork chops for 24 hours.
- Pre-heat water bath to your ideal temperature. We prefer 140°F.
- Vacuum seal the pork or put it in a heavy duty Ziploc bag using the water displacement method.
- Put packaged pork chop in water bath and cook for 1.5 - 3 hours.
- Take out pork chop and pat dry with paper towels.
- Pre-heat cast iron pan on medium-high heat and add avocado oil (or high smoke point oil).
- Sear on hot cast iron pan using for 1 minute, flipping every 15 seconds.

- Add butter and any aromatics to the pan for additional flavor and crispness. Sear for an additional 30 or so.

- (Optional) Break out the searing torch if you're feeling adventurous for a perfect crust.

- If you want, serve with pan sauce made from bag juices and remaining marinade.

CHAPTER TWENTY THREE
SOUS VIDE SHORT RIBS

Beef short ribs have the largest array of possible textures and flavor profiles out of any meat cooked sous vide. A 72 hour cook at 130F delivers a texture you've never experienced before, while 24 hours at 165F delivers a traditional yet juicy texture. This is absolutely one of the most transformational uses of sous vide.

Ingredients

- Beef Short Ribs (2-4)
- Sea Salt
- Cracked Black Pepper
- Garlic Powder
- Avocado Oil (or another high smoke point oil)

How to prepare

- Usually an elective step of marinating beforehand, but because this recipe cooks for a minimum of 24 hours, the beef will marinate in its juices and whatever spices you add - perfect!

- Pre-heat water bath to your ideal temperature. We recommend 165°F for a traditional, yet juicy, texture; however, the famous 72 hour short rib is also a masterpiece.

- Generously season with sea salt, cracked black pepper, a pinch of garlic powder, and any aromatics such as rosemary or thyme.

- Vacuum seal the short ribs. Or if you're cooking the 48 hour or 72 hour recipe, you can place it in a heavy duty Ziploc bag using the water displacement method since the temperatures are low enough. Temperatures over 155F can break the seal of Ziploc bags.

- Remove ribs and pat dry with paper towels, saving the juice from the bag.

- Using a cheese cloth, filter the juice into a saucepan and lessen by half at a simmer.

- Pre-heat cast iron pan on medium-high heat and add avocado oil (or another high smoke point oil).

- Sear ribs on hot cast iron pan for about 1 minute, flipping every 15 seconds.

- Add butter and any aromatics to the pan for added flavor and crispness. Sear for an

- (Optional) Break out the searing torch if you're feeling adventurous for a perfect crust.

- Plate beef short ribs with juice reduction.

CHAPTER TWENTY FOUR
SOUS VIDE SAUSAGE

Sous vide sausage is unbelievably juicy and is one of the only meats that taste awesome right from the bag without having to worry about searing.

Ingredients

- Sausage

- (Optional) Beer, Beef Stock

How to prepare

- Pre-heat water bath to 160F depending on your preference. 140F will be very juicy and soft, 150F will be juicy and firm, 160F will be like the conventional but still more juicy.

- Vacuum seal your sausage or use Ziploc freezer bags with the water displacement method. (Optional) if you plan on eating the sausage plain and/or on a bun, you can add a light beer and some beef broth to your bag during the cook.

- Cook for 1-2 hours.

- Take out sausage from bag, discard juices, and pat dry with paper towels.

- If eating as an appetizer or on a bun, you can quickly sear it on a grill or cast iron. However, sous vide sausage is one of few meats that taste great right from the bag!

CHAPTER TWENTY FIVE
SOUS VIDE HALIBUT

Halibut is traditionally a firm fish, which makes it great for searing. Since the fish is normally pretty firm, it also tends to become really dry with conventional cooking methods. Sous vide lets you ensure the halibut stays absolutely moist and flaky, while still being able to obtain an amazing golden brown sear.

Ingredients

- 2 Halibut Filets; I ordered mine from Omaha Steaks.
- 2 tbs.Butter
- Fresh Dill
- Lemon
- Salt
- Pepper
- Olive Oil

Temperature

[140F for 45 minutes] Traditional texture (a bit tougher) much more dry than the temperatures below.

[130F for 45 minutes] It is moist but still firm enough to sear it without worrying about it falling apart.

[120F for 45 minutes] Most tender, but still nearly raw.

How to prepare

- Dry brine halibut by richly salting both sides (and use a 50/50 ratio of salt/sugar) and place back in refrigerator for at least 30 minutes or up to 24 hours.

- Preheat water bath to your desired temperature shown above; I prefer 130F.

- Carefully place the halibut filets in a Ziploc bag. Add in a bit of oil and fresh dill to the bag. Place into the water bath using the water displacement technique.

- Cook for 45 minutes, or about an hour and 15 minutes if frozen.

- Take out from water bath and tenderly pat the halibut dry with paper towels. This is crucial for obtaining a nice quick sear.

- Pre-heat a cast iron or stainless steel pan with avocado oil on medium-high/high heat.

- Add halibut, followed by a tablespoon or two of butter and fresh herbs.

- Baste the halibut with butter as it cooks, 1-2 minutes (you only need to sear the one side).

- Remove and serve!

CHAPTER TWENTY SIX
SOUS VIDE POACHED EGGS + AVOCADO TOAST

This worthy breakfast is just as healthy as it is tasty, and sous vide makes poached eggs a breeze. In just 15 minutes, you can have constantly perfect, gooey eggs, every single time.

Ingredients

- 2 - 4 Eggs
- Avocado Toast
- 2 slices of bread, toasted (I prefer rye)
- 1 Avocado, sliced or spread on bread (if you opt to slice instead of spread, I recommend spreading some butter on the toast)
- Salt (I like to use a chili lime sea salt)
- Pepper
- Chives

How to prepare

- Preheat water bath to 167F
- Gently lower your eggs into the water, ensuring not to crack. I use a pair of kitchen tongs.
- Cook for 15 minutes.

- Remove eggs and run them under cold tap water for 30 seconds or so to prevent them from overcooking.

- Place avocado on toast and top with salt, pepper, and chives.

- Gently crack an egg or two over your toast and enjoy!

CHAPTER TWENTY SEVEN
SOUS VIDE COD

Cod (and salmon) do not require a finishing sear once it's done cooking, so it can't get any easier! Just bag the cod filets with some butter, dill, lemon, and capers, and cook for 45 minutes. You can even melt your serving butter right in the water bath along with the fish!

Ingredients

- 2 Cod Filets
- 2 tbs. Butter
- Fresh Dill
- (Optional) Lemon and Capers
- Salt
- Pepper

How to prepare

- Preheat water bath to your desired temperature shown above; I prefer 130F.
- Gently place the cod filets in a Ziploc bag. Add in 2tbps of butter and some fresh dill to the bag. Optionally, you can also add a few slices of lemon and capers into the bag.

- Put bag into the water bath using the water displacement method.

- Cook for 45 minutes, or about an hour and 15 minutes if frozen.

- Take it out and serve! Cod, much like salmon, does not require a sear like most meats we cook sous vide.

CHAPTER TWENTY EIGHT
SOUS VIDE COLD BREW COFFEE

Thanks to sous vide, cold brew coffee no longer needs to take 24 hours to make! We can cut the brewing time down to 2 hours and have the same tasting results. Give this sous vide cold brew coffee recipe a try!

Ingredients

- 3/4 Cup Fresh, Coarsely Ground Coffee
- 4 Cups of Water
- 2 16oz Mason Jars (or smaller sizes equaling to 32oz)

How to prepare

- Grind your fresh coffee beans on a very coarse setting - finely ground coffee can end up cloudy when cold brewing.
- Pour the coffee grounds and water to a large bowl and stir until all coffee grounds are soaked.
- Equally pour the coffee mixture into your mason jars ensuring to leave at least a half inch of room from the top.
- Put the lids on the mason jars and ONLY tighten with your finger tips. Over-tightening the lid can break the glass, as air needs to escape when heating.

- Immerse the mason jars into a pre-heated water bath at 150F for about 2 hours.

- Take out jars, filter the coffee with either a coffee filter or cheese cloth, and chill in the fridge.

- (Optional) The coffee will be quite strong as is - if it's too strong for your tastes, dilute the coffee by adding more cold water, up to a 1:1 ratio.

- Pour and serve over ice!

CHAPTER TWENTY NINE
SOUS VIDE GARLIC HERB BUTTER STEAK

These steaks are so delicious, juicy and evenly cooked. Sous vide is a really exciting method to explore as a home cook.

Ingredients

- 4 Filet Mignon Steaks about 1/2 pound each
- Kosher salt
- Freshly ground pepper
- Garlic powder
- 2 tablespoons of butter
- 1 clove of garlic finely minced
- 2 tablespoons of chopped fresh flat leaf parsley
- 1-2 tablespoon of vegetable oil

How to prepare

- Season steaks to taste with salt, pepper and a small amount of garlic powder.
- Heat Sous Vide to temperature based on preference of doneness, from rare, medium-rare or medium. Refer to chart in directions for temp and time guidelines.

- If preference is medium-rare, heat water bath to 130 degrees to account for increase in temp during final searing and set timer for one hour.

- When water is heated, submerge steaks in plastic storage bag and seal.

- While steaks are cooking, prepare garlic butter.

- Mix softened butter with minced garlic, pinch of salt and parsley.

- Remove steaks from water bath after one hour.

- Heat cast iron skillet over high heat with 1-2 tablespoon of olive oil. Once oil is smoking, quickly sear steaks on each side. 30 second to 1 minute per side.

- Top the steaks with butter compound, let it rest and serve.

CHAPTER THIRTY
SOUS VIDE CARROTS

Cooking carrots sous vide prevents all the flavor and nutrients leaching out, resulting in crunchy, flavorsome carrots every time.

Ingredients

- Carrot
- Olive oil
- Salt

How to prepare

- Preheat the water bath to 85°C
- Place a single layer of baby carrots in a vacuum bag and add a little olive oil and a pinch of salt
- Vacuum seal the bag and place it in the preheated water bath to cook for 25 minutes
- Take out the carrots from the bag and drain on kitchen paper. Serve immediately with a knob of butter

CHAPTER THIRTY ONE
SOUS VIDE LAMB CHOPS WITH BASIL CHIMICHURRI

Ingredients:

Lamb chops

- 2 rack of lamb, frenched
- 2 cloves garlic, crushed
- Salt
- pepper

Basil Chimichurri

- 1 cup fresh basil, finely chopped
- 1 shallot diced
- 1-2 clove of garlic, minced
- 1 ts red chili flakes
- 1/2 olive oil
- 3 tbs. red wine vinegar
- 1/4 tbs.sea salt
- 1/4 tbs. pepper

How to prepare

- Set sous vide temperature to 56 degrees Celsius. Season lamb liberally with salt and pepper. Vacuum seal lamb with crush garlic and sous vide for 2 hours.

- Combine all of the ingredients of the basil chimichurri sauce in bowl and mix well. Season to taste and cover and refrigerate to let flavors blend together.

- After two hours, remove lamb chops from bag and dry well with paper towel. Sear with torch or scalding hot well oiled pan. Slice the between the bones and liberally top with basil chimichurri sauce and enjoy.

CHAPTER THIRTY TWO
SOUS VIDE DUCK LEGS

Ingredients

- 4 duck legs
- Kosher salt and freshly ground black pepper
- 4 medium cloves garlic, minced
- 4 sprigs thyme

How to prepare

- Set up an immersion circulator and preheat the water bath to 155°F (68°C).
- Season duck all over with salt and pepper. Rub garlic onto the meaty side of each leg and set a thyme sprig on top. Slide duck legs into vacuum bags and seal according to vacuum-sealer manufacturer's instructions.
- Add sealed duck to water bath and cook for 36 hours. Make sure to top water up periodically as it evaporates, and keep bag totally underwater. If bag floats, weigh it down by placing a wet kitchen towel on top of it.
- Take out duck from water bath and transfer to a refrigerator to chill. The duck can be kept refrigerated within the sealed bag for up to 1 week.

- When ready to use, take out duck from bag and scrape away thyme sprigs and excess fat and juices. Use duck confit according to any recipe you have; it can be cooked in a 450°F (230°C) oven or broiled until the meat is heated through and the skin is browned and crispy, about 7 minutes.

CHAPTER THIRTY THREE
SOUS VIDE SPICED AUBERGINE WITH TURMERIC AND COCONUT SAUCE, CASHEW BUTTER AND CRISPY KALE

Ingredients

Sous vide aubergine

- 6 baby aubergines
- 1/2 tsp coriander seeds
- 1/2 tsp fennel seeds
- 1/2 tsp cumin seeds
- 50ml of olive oil
- table salt
- sea salt
- freshly ground black pepper

Kale crisps

- 200g of kale
- 1 tbsp of olive oil
- 1 tbsp of cashew nuts
- table salt

Turmeric and coconut sauce

- 20g of fresh turmeric, sliced
- 2 shallots, sliced
- 1 knob of ginger, 3cm in length, peeled and sliced
- 20g of cashew nuts, toasted
- 1/4 bunch of coriander stalks
- 400ml of coconut milk
- 1 dash of vegetable oil

Cashew butter

- 100g of cashew nuts, toasted
- 100ml of warm water
- Salt

How to prepare

For the kale crisps, rub the oil into the leaves and season well with table salt. Microplane the cashew nuts over the kale and place in a dehydrator or 60°C oven overnight to crisp up

- For the aubergine, preheat the water bath to 72°C
- Put the coriander, fennel and cumin seeds in a dry frying pan over a medium heat and toast until it is fragrant, lightly crush and mix with the olive oil

- Halve the aubergines lengthwise and score the flesh in a crisscross pattern. Season it generously with table salt and leave for 10 minutes. After 10 minutes, wipe away the salt and any excess moisture

- Put the aubergines in 2 vacuum bags and add the spiced oil. Seal, being careful not to take all of the air out as you will crush the aubergines, and place in the water bath for 90 minutes

- For the turmeric and coconut sauce, heat a dash of vegetable oil in a large saucepan. When hot, add all the ingredients apart from the coconut milk. Season well, cook for 10 minutes until lightly colored then add the coconut milk

- Simmer for 20 minutes then place in a blender and blitz until smooth. Pass through a fine sieve

- For the cashew butter, place the cashew nuts in a blender, season well and add the warm water. Blend until smooth, adding a little more water if necessary. Transfer to a piping bag

- Remove the aubergines from the bags and season with a little sea salt and pepper

- Plate the aubergines with dots of cashew butter, drizzles of turmeric sauce and pieces of crispy kale

CHAPTER THIRTY FOUR
SOUS VIDE BRUSSELS SPROUTS AND SPROUT TOPS, MISO BUTTER, CASHEW

Ingredients

- 16 Brussels sprouts
- 1kg sprout tops, hard stalks removed
- 2 bay leaves
- 30g miso paste
- 100g unsalted butter
- 80g roasted cashew nuts, chopped
- 1 tbsp chopped tarragon leaves

How to prepare

- Preheat your water to 70^0C 1
- Start by making the miso butter. Tip the miso paste into a bowl along with the butter and whisk together.
- Prep the sprouts by chopping off the bottom and if large, cut in half so that they are all approximately the same size. Move the sprouts to a vacuum bag along with a couple of bay leaves and half of the miso butter.

- Vacuum seal the pouch and pop into the water bath to sous vide for 45 minutes. 4

- Place the sprout tops into a separate vacuum bag along with the remaining half of the miso butter. Seal and put into the water bath for the last 20 minutes of cooking.

- To arrange the dish, take the cooked sprouts from the bath and mix in a bowl with the cashew nuts and tarragon leaves.

CHAPTER THIRTY FIVE
SOUS VIDE LEEKS

Cooking leeks can be difficult because the outer layers cook faster than the inner core. This makes it hard to achieve a uniform result. You can avoid this problem by cooking leeks sous vide in a water bath. In this technique, the low cooking temperature means that the leeks never go beyond the optimum temperature, which prevents them from overcooking on the outside.

Ingredients

- 3 large leeks, trimmed with base intact
- 25ml of olive oil
- salt

How to prepare

- Preheat the water bath to a temperature of 85^0C. 1
- Arrange the leeks side by side in a vacuum bag. Season it with salt, pour over the olive oil and vacuum the bag to seal
- Put the bag in the water bath and leave it to cook for around 30 minutes. To test if the leeks are cooked, give them a gentle squeeze; if they feel tender, they are ready.

- Slide the leeks out of the vacuum bag and drain it on kitchen paper

CHAPTER THIRTY SIX
POLENTA SOUS VIDE

If you are looking for a delicious substitute to wheat or potato, polenta – at times known as cornmeal – is a great choice. However, cooking polenta in the conventional way using a saucepan can be difficult: the polenta can stick to the base of the pan and, unless it is stirred very frequently, it can form a horrible skin. You can evade these common problems by cooking polenta sous vide.

How to prepare

- Preheat the water bath to a temperature of 85^0C.

- Position the polenta in a large bowl and add the water, butter and parmesan. Stir until thoroughly combined.

- Seal the mixture inside a vacuum bag.

- Put the bag in the water bath and leave it to cook for 2 hours.

- Tip the cooked polenta out of the vacuum bag into a bowl. It is now ready to be served.

CHAPTER THIRTY SEVEN
SOUS VIDE FENNEL AND ORANGE QUINOA SALAD

Ingredients

Quinoa and fennel salad

- 100g of quinoa
- 500ml of vegetable stock
- 1 fennel bulb, cut into eighths
- 50ml of orange juice
- 1 pinch of saffron
- 2 tbsp of pomegranate seeds
- 1 tsp sesame seeds, toasted
- 2 tsp fresh coriander, finely chopped
- 3 tbsp of extra virgin olive oil
- 1 tbsp of lemon vinegar
- salt
- freshly ground black pepper

Toasted pine nuts

- 2 tsp pine nuts
- 1 pinch of salt

Tahini Dressing

- 1 tbsp of tahini
- 20ml of lemon juice
- 50ml of olive oil
- 6 orange segments
- nasturtium leaves
- coriander cress

How to prepare

- First, cook the quinoa. Put the quinoa in a medium sized saucepan and pour over the vegetable stock. Heat until the stock reaches the boil, then simmer until the quinoa is cooked al dente. This should take around 15 minutes. Once cooked, take the pan off the heat and set aside to cool.

- Preheat the water bath to a temperature of 85°C.

- To prepare the fennel, seal the fennel wedges inside a vacuum bag with the orange juice and the saffron. Place the bag in the water bath and leave to cook for 20 minutes.

- Unseal and drain the vacuum bag. Lay the cooked fennel in a hot frying pan. Cook over a high heat until browned on one side, then turn over and brown the other side. Add the seared fennel to the quinoa and mix in the pomegranate seeds, toasted sesame seeds and chopped coriander.

- Prepare a lemon dressing for the salad by thoroughly combining the olive oil and lemon vinegar in a small bowl. Drizzle a small amount of dressing over the quinoa, followed by a sprinkling of salt and pepper, and mix well. Taste the salad to check the flavor and seasoning. If desired, add a little more dressing.

- To make the toasted pine nuts, warm a frying pan over a low heat. Scatter the pine nuts over the base of the pan and fry gently until lightly toasted all over. To season, add a pinch of salt to the pan and shake vigorously.

- Just before serving, make the tahini dressing. Place the tahini, lemon juice and olive oil in a small bowl and mix together using a whisk.

- To serve, spoon an equal amount of quinoa and fennel salad onto each plate. Scatter the toasted pine nuts, orange segments, nasturtium leaves and coriander cress over the salad, then finish the dish with a drizzle of tahini dressing.

CHAPTER THIRTY EIGHT
BEETROOT WITH PICKLED QUINCE

Ingredients

Quince pickles

- 1 quince, peeled
- 250g of white balsamic vinegar
- 250g of Chardonnay vinegar
- 230g of water
- 1 sprig of lemon verbena
- Cheltenham beetroot
- 4 Cheltenham beetroot
- 25g of olive oil
- 1 sprig of thyme
- salt
- pepper

Marinated beetroot

- 1 baby golden beetroot
- 1 baby white beetroot

- 16 spinach leaves
- 1 handful of chervil
- olive oil
- salt

How to prepare

- To prepare the pickled quince, mix the white balsamic vinegar, Chardonnay vinegar, water and lemon verbena in a saucepan and heat it until the mixture reaches the boil, then allow to cool slightly. Place the quince in a vacuum bag and pour over the warm pickling liquid. Vacuum the bag in a chamber sealer and set aside for 24 hours to pickle.

- Preheat the oven to a temperature of 180°C/gas mark 4.

- Rub the Cheltenham beetroot with olive oil and season it with salt and pepper, then arrange it on a baking tray and scatter over the thyme.

- Put the baking tray in the oven and cook until the beetroot are heated through but still firm. This should take about 30 minutes. Once cooked, take the tray out of the oven. Set aside to cool a little, then peel the beetroot, reserving the skins, and slice the flesh into thirds.

- In a blender, purée the skins from the Cheltenham beetroot. Put the purée in a covered container and keep warm until ready to serve.

- To make the marinated beetroot, cut the baby beetroot into thin slices. Unseal the vacuum bag containing the quince and remove the fruit, then pour the pickling liquid over the sliced beetroot and leave to marinate.

- Finely dice the pickled quince.

- When you are ready to serve, heat a dash of olive oil in a saucepan, add the spinach leaves and gently sauté until just wilted. Sprinkle a pinch of salt over the wilted leaves to season.

- To serve, smear a spoonful or two of beetroot purée over the base of each plate and top with one of the Cheltenham beetroot. Scatter the diced quince and marinated baby beetroot around the plate, add 4 spinach leaves and finish with a garnish of chervil sprigs.

CHAPTER THIRTY NINE
SOUS VIDE POTATO RÖSTI

Ingredients

- 2kg Maris Piper potatoes, grated
- 120g of duck fat, plus extra for pan-frying
- salt, to season generously

How to prepare

- Preheat the water bath to a temperature of $80^\circ C$.

- Throw the grated potato with the salt, then put in a colander and set aside to drain. The salt will draw out the starchy water in potato.

- After 15 minutes, wrap the potato in a clean, dry tea towel. Twist the tea towel until you cannot squeeze out any more moisture, then move the potato to a mixing bowl.

- Heat the duck fat in a small saucepan until it is completely melted. Tip the molten fat into the bowl with the grated potato and stir until thoroughly mixed, then seal the mixture in a large vacuum bag using a chamber sealer.

- Put the bag in the water bath and cook for 4 hours.

- Once it is cooked, leave the potato to cool inside the vacuum bag. When it has cooled completely, unseal the bag, remove the rösti and divide into 8 portions. You can make the portions any shape you choose.

- Melt some duck fat in a frying pan; add the portions of rösti and fry, turning as necessary, until golden brown and crispy all over.

CHAPTER FORTY
PUMPKIN VELOUTÉ WITH WILD MUSHROOMS

Ingredients

- 1kg pumpkin
- 100g of butter
- 10ml of truffle oil
- salt

Wild mushrooms

- 250g of girolles mushrooms
- vegetable oil
- 1 knob of butter
- sea salt
- 10g of chives, chopped
- pumpkin seeds, roasted – to serve
- truffle, grated – to serve

How to prepare

- Preheat the water bath to a temperature of 90°C.

- To make the pumpkin, remove its outer skin, then cut the flesh into wedges and scoop out the seeds.

- Slice the wedges on a mandoline to make thin slivers of pumpkin. Season it with salt, and then seal half the pumpkin slivers, butter and truffle oil in one vacuum bag and half in another. Place both vacuum bags in the water bath and leave to cook for 90 minutes.

- Move the cooked pumpkin into a blender and pulse to make a smooth and glossy velouté. If the velouté is very thick, loosen it with a splash of water. Add salt to taste and store it in a warm place until needed. Do not allow the velouté to cool.

- Rinse the mushrooms in plenty of cold water, then leave to drain on kitchen paper. When the mushrooms are clean and dry, carefully strip the skin off the stems with a small knife.

- In very hot frying pan, fry the mushrooms with a dash of oil until it is lightly browned, and then stir in the butter, flaky sea salt and chopped chives.

- To serve, put a few mushrooms in the centre of each bowl, keeping about a third in reserve. Spoon the velouté into the bowls, then finish the dish by scattering the roasted pumpkin seeds, grated truffle and remaining mushrooms over the top.

CHAPTER FORTY ONE
PICKLED RADISH, DILL EMULSION AND PUFFED QUINOA

Ingredients

Dill emulsion

- 3 bunches of dill
- 300ml of sunflower oil
- 50ml of cider vinegar
- 3 egg yolks
- salt to season

Dill powder

- 1 bunch of dill

Quinoa

- 100g of quinoa
- 500ml of vegetable oil

Pickled radishes

- 1 bunch of radishes
- 200ml of white wine vinegar

- 100ml of water
- 50g of sugar

How to prepare

- To make the dill emulsion, begin by blanching the dill in boiling water then shocking it in cold water to stop the cooking process.
- Dry the dill as thoroughly as possible. Mix with the oil and liquidize in a blender.
- Suspend a muslin bag over a large jug. Pour the dill oil into the bag and leave it to strain into the jug overnight.
- Next, make the dill powder. To do this, place the dill in a dehydrator. Leave it to dry for 3 hours then take it out from the dehydrator and reduce it to a fine powder with the use of a blender.
- Bring a large pan of water to the boil and add in the quinoa. Simmer it until it is soft, then refresh the quinoa in cold water and place it in a dehydrator. Dry until it is crispy.
- To pickle the radishes, place them in a vacuum bag. Combine the white wine vinegar, water and sugar and pour over the radishes, then seal the bag using a chamber sealer. Leave to pickle for 1 hour, then open the bag, drain off the pickling liquid and set the radishes to one side.

- To finish up the dill emulsion, combine together the cider vinegar and egg yolk with the use of a whisk. When they are thoroughly combined, very gradually add the dill oil. Keep whisking until all the oil has been added and the mixture is smooth and emulsified. Add salt to taste.

- Preheat a deep-fryer to a temperature of $210\,^{\circ}\mathrm{C}$. When this temperature has been reached, add the dehydrated quinoa and fry until golden.

- To serve it, divide the pickled radishes between two plates. Pour some of the dill emulsion onto each plate, scatter the quinoa over the top and finish with a dusting of dill powder.

CHAPTER FORTY TWO
SOUS VIDE PIGS EARS

Pig's ears are a sadly underrated and the most underused part of the pig. Cooked properly, they are a very delicious savory treat and, when fried and crispy, they make a great canape. Furthermore, because the demand is low, they are usually very cheap, although you may have to order them in advance from your butcher.

Ingredients

- 4 pig's ears
- 50g of rock salt
- 50ml of vegetable oil
- Rice flour, for dusting

How to prepare

- Rinse the pig's ears thoroughly in cold running water then dry it using kitchen paper.
- Rub the salt into the ears. Set aside to cure for 6 hours.
- Preheat the water bath to a temperature of 85^0C.
- Rinse the pig's ears again, getting rid of as much of the salt as possible, then seal it in a vacuum bag with the oil.

- Place the bag in the water bath and leave to cook for 12 hours. Remove the bag from the bath and set aside to cool.

- Once the ears have cooled to room temperature, remove them from the bag, pat dry and place in the fridge until thoroughly chilled.

- Slice the cold pig's ears into strips 1cm in thickness then sprinkle with a dusting of rice flour.

- Heat some oil to a temperature of 190°C, then add the pig's ears and fry until crispy. This should take around 2 minutes.

CHAPTER FORTY THREE
SUCKLING PIG WITH CHOU FARCI, HUMMUS AND CHICKPEA FRICASSEE

Ingredients

- 250g of suckling pig loin
- Suckling pig belly
- 250g of suckling pig belly, boned
- 1 sprig of thyme, chopped
- 1 sprig of rosemary, chopped
- salt

Suckling pig sauce

- 1kg suckling pig bones
- 1l chicken stock
- 100g of onion
- 100g of carrots
- 100g of celery
- 100g of leek
- 1 garlic

- 2 sprigs of thyme
- 30g of tomato purée
- 100ml of red wine
- 50g of butter, cubed

Chou farci

- 250g of suckling pig leg, deboned
- 25g of smoked bacon
- 6 savoy cabbage leaves

Pickled onions

- 125ml of white wine vinegar
- 125g of sugar
- 125g of silver skin onion
- 2 black peppercorns
- 1 star anise
- 2 cloves
- 1 bay leaf

Hummus

- 400g of chickpeas

- 3 garlic cloves
- 75ml of olive oil
- 1 tsp smoked paprika
- 3 tsp lemon juice
- 1 tsp sugar
- 125g of tahini
- 1 tsp ground cumin
- salt

Charred leeks

- 2 leeks

Chickpea fricassee

- 100g of chickpeas
- 1 shallot, finely diced
- 1 garlic clove, finely diced
- 1 tsp chopped chives
- 20ml of lemon juice
- 10g of butter
- salt

How to prepare

- To prepare the suckling pig belly, preheat the water bath to a temperature of 85°C.

- Mix together the salt, chopped thyme and chopped rosemary and massage into the belly.

- Seal the seasoned meat inside a large vacuum bag using a bar sealer.

- Place the bag in the water bath and leave to cook sous vide for 7 hours.

- Unseal the vacuum bag and remove the belly. Pat the meat dry on kitchen paper, then place in a shallow tray lined with baking parchment.

- Cover the meat with another layer of baking parchment and balance a second tray on top.

- Weigh down the top tray with something heavy, then leave to press in the fridge until chilled through.

- Preheat the oven to a temperature of 180°C/gas mark 4.

- For the suckling pig sauce, place the bones in a roasting dish and cook in the oven until caramelized. This should take approximately 1 hour.

- Heat a splash of oil in a large saucepan, then add the onion, carrot, celery and leek and brown over a high heat.

- When the vegetables are well-colored, stir in the tomato purée, thyme and roasted bones and add enough chicken stock to cover all of the ingredients completely.

- Simmer for 3 hours, pouring in extra stock when necessary to keep the bones covered.

- After this time, strain the sauce through 3 layers of muslin cloth, then place a clean pan and mix in the red wine.

- Cook over a medium heat until reduced to 1/3 of the original volume. When it is ready, the mixture will be sauce-like in consistency.

- Next, make the chou farci. Grind the suckling pig leg and the smoked bacon together in a mincer, then add a splash of the suckling pig sauce and mix well. Keep adding sauce until the mince binds together, then add a pinch of salt and refrigerate for 1 hour.

- After this time, take the meat out of the fridge and divide into 40g pieces. Roll each piece into a ball and arrange on a tray. Place the tray in the fridge and leave to set.

- Bring a saucepan of salted water to the boil and add the cabbage leaves. Simmer for 2 minutes, then remove the leaves and plunge into iced water to halt the cooking process. Leave to drain on kitchen paper.

- Place one of the blanched cabbage leaves on a sheet of cling film and top with a chilled ball of farci. Fold the cabbage over the meat until it is completely encased, then stretch the cling film around the ball to secure the leaf in place.

- Repeat step 15 with rest of the cabbage leaves and meat balls, then place the chou farci in the fridge and leave to set for a minimum of 30 minutes.

- Preheat the water bath to a temperature of 55°C.

- To prepare the sucking pig loin, remove the sinew and chop the meat into 40g slices.

- Seasons the slices with salt, then use a bar sealer to seal each one in a separate vacuum bag with a little oil.

- Place the bags in the water bath and leave to sous vide for 30 minutes.

- Next, pickle the onions. In a large saucepan, combine the water, vinegar, sugar, peppercorns, star anise, cloves and bay leaf. Heat until the liquid boils and the sugar dissolves completely, and then tip the hot mixture over the onions. Set aside until cool.

- When the onions are cool, remove their skins and return them to the pickling liquid. Leave to pickle until needed.

- Preheat the oven to a temperature of 120°C/gas mark 1/4.

- Take the chou farci out of the fridge, remove the cling film and place on a baking sheet in the oven. Cook for

- 10 minutes, then dip the balls in the suckling pig sauce and leave in a warm place until required.

- For the hummus, mix the chickpeas, garlic cloves, olive oil, paprika, lemon juice, sugar, tahini, cumin and salt in a blender. Add 175ml of hot water and pulse the blender until the mixture becomes smooth.

- To make the charred leeks, fill a saucepan with salted water and bring to the boil. Add the leeks and simmer until they are just cooked. This should take about 5 minutes. Once it is cooked, plunge the leeks into iced water, then leave it on kitchen paper to drain.

- Slice the leeks into 6 equal lengths and put it in hot frying pan. Do not add any oil or cooking fat. Fry the leeks until they are caramelized, then leave in warm place until it is ready to serve.

- Next, make the fricassee. Heat the butter in a small saucepan. When it has completely melted, add the shallot and garlic and sauté over a gentle heat until softened but not colored.

- Mix in the chickpeas and 2 tbsp of the pickled onions. Continue to cook for another 2 minutes, and then add the lemon juice, salt and chives to finish.

- Take the suckling pig belly out of the fridge and take out the weighted tray. Slice the meat into individual portions and place to one side.

- Unseal the vacuum bags containing the suckling pig loin. Take out the meat and pat dry with kitchen paper. At the same time, heat a dash of oil in a frying pan.

- When the oil is hot, add in the loin and caramelize over a medium heat, then set aside to rest, leaving the pan on the heat.

- Arrange the belly slices cut-side down in the hot pan and quickly sear the meat. Turn the slices over and sear the other cut surfaces, then take out from the pan.

- To serve, abundantly smear the base of each plate with hummus and top up with a few spoonfuls of chickpea fricassee. Arrange 1 portion of pork belly, 1 slice of pork loin and 1 ball of chou farci in a line across the centre of the plate, then add 2 pieces of charred leek. Drizzle the warm suckling pig sauce atop the meat and finish the dish with a garnish of puffed pork rind and celery cress.

CHAPTER FORTY FOUR
SOUS VIDE PORK BELLY

Even though it is a relatively cheap cut of meat, pork belly can be succulent and tender if it is treated with care. Low temperatures and long cooking times are important to prevent the meat from drying out and losing its flavor. Pork belly is therefore perfectly suited to being cooked sous vide as this technique allows you to maintain consistently low temperatures over long periods.

Ingredients

- 1kg pork belly
- 2 liters water
- 100g salt

How to prepare

- To ensure even seasoning, brine the pork before cooking. Add the salt to the water and stir until it is dissolved. Put the pork in the water, ensuring that it is totally submerged. Set it aside to brine for 6 hours.
- Preheat the water bath to a temperature of $64^\circ C$.
- Take out the pork from the brine, put inside a vacuum bag and seal.
- Place the bag in the water bath and leave it to cook for 24 hours.

- Take the pork out of the bag and pat with kitchen paper to dry, draining off any juices as you do so.

- Move the pork to a tray then put another tray and a heavy weight on top. Rest it in the fridge for a minimum of 6 hours. If possible, leave it overnight.

- Take out the pork from between the two trays and slice it into individual portions. Heat a little oil in a frying pan then add the pork and fry, turning as necessary, until it is crisp and golden on both sides.

CHAPTER FORTY FIVE
PORK SHOULDER WITH HISPI CABBAGE AND APPLES

Ingredients

- 1.4kg pork shoulder
- 14g of salt

Apple and celeriac purée

- 500g of Bramley apple, peeled, cored and sliced
- 25g of olive oil
- 1/2 tsp lemon juice
- 200g of celeriac, peeled and sliced
- 200ml of milk
- 1 pinch of salt
- 1 tsp cider vinegar

Pork sauce

- 1.2kg pork bones
- 800ml of chicken stock
- 400g of pork trimmings

SOUS VIDE COOKBOOK

- 400ml of white wine
- 200g of button mushrooms, sliced
- lemon zest, 1 piece
- 1 lemon juice
- 1 garlic clove
- 1 sprig of fresh thyme
- 1.2g of xanthan gum
- 1 tsp Chardonnay vinegar
- 1 pinch of black pepper

Hispi cabbage

- 1 Hispi cabbage
- 10ml of white wine vinegar
- 20ml of duck fat

Red apple slices

- 2 Redlove apples, sliced
- 125ml of lemon juice
- 250ml of water
- 250ml of sugar

How to prepare

- Preheat the water bath to a temperature of 70°C.

- Debone the pork shoulder and rub the salt into meat. Shape the joint into an oblong, then stretch cling film around the meat to make sure it holds the shape. Seal inside a vacuum bag with the use of a chamber sealer.

- Put the bag in the water bath and leave to cook for 12 hours. After this time, move the meat to the fridge and leave it overnight to chill.

- Preheat the water bath to a temperature of 88°C.

- For the apple and celeriac purée, seal the sliced apple and celeriac in a vacuum bag with the olive oil. You will need to use a chamber sealer to do this.

- Put the bag in the water bath and leave it to cook sous vide. After 30 minutes, take out the bag and place the contents in a blender with the lemon juice, milk, salt and cider vinegar. Pulse the mixture in the blender until it is smooth.

- Preheat the oven to a temperature of 180°C/gas mark 4.

- Next, prepare the pork sauce. Arrange the pork bones on a baking tray and place in the oven. Cook it until it is golden brown.

- Heat the chicken stock in a large saucepan. When the stock is boiling, tip the roasted pork bones into the pan and simmer for 1 hour. Put the white wine in a separate saucepan over a medium heat. Cook for 10 minutes, starting the clock when the wine reaches the boil, then set aside until needed.

- Brown the pork trimmings in a big saucepan. When the trimmings have caramelized, empty the meat and fat from the pan into a colander and leave it to drain.

- Pass the stock through a fine sieve to take out the bones, and then place in a clean saucepan with the caramelized trimmings, the button mushrooms and the garlic. Bring to the boil and cook over a gentle heat for 1 hour.

- Strain the sauce through a fine sieve and leave to settle then get rid of any fat that has come to surface. Stir in the xanthan gum to thicken the sauce, add salt and pepper to taste and mix in the lemon juice and vinegar. Infuse the sauce with the thyme sprig and the lemon rind for 20 minutes then set aside until needed.

- Next, prepare the hispi cabbage. Shred the hispi cabbage into long thin strips. Melt the duck fat in a saucepan and add in the cabbage. Sauté until tender, then add salt to season and mix in the vinegar.

- To make the red apple slices, mix the sugar, water and lemon juice in a saucepan. Immerse the apple slices in the mixture and heat until boiling then simmer for 4 minutes. After this time, drain off the liquid and set the apple aside until it is needed.

- For the parsnips, bring a saucepan of salted water to the boil. Add the parsnips and simmer for 3½ minutes.

- Preheat the water bath to a temperature of 62°C.

- Seal the pork shoulder inside a neat vacuum bag using a chamber sealer. Put in the water bath and sous vide for 15 minutes until reheated all the way through. Unseal the bag and pat the meat dry on kitchen paper.

- Put the shoulder skin-side down in a hot frying pan and fry until the skin is crispy. After frying, check that the meat is hot all the way through by inserting a skewer into the centre, then cut into 4 portions.

- To serve, split the hispi cabbage among 4 plates. Heap the cabbage into a pile in the centre of each plate and top with a portion of pork shoulder. Put 2 slices of apple beside the cabbage and dot the plate with apple and celeriac purée. Spoon the pork sauce over the meat and finish each plate with 2 baby parsnips.

CHAPTER FORTY SIX
TEQUILA CHICKEN

Tequila, it makes you happy, oh tequila……..they say that is how the song goes!! A bit cheeky for a Monday tea time but let's see what you think! Try this tasty tequila chicken.

Ingredients

- 2 chicken breast halves, boneless and skinless
- Salt, to taste
- Black pepper, to taste
- 2 tablespoons (10 ml) butter
- 2 tablespoons (10 ml) tequila
- 1 lime, for juice
- Fresh chives, chopped, for garnish

How to prepare

- Fill and preheat your water bath to 63.5C.
- Lightly season the chicken breasts with salt and pepper, place into a small (quart/0.9 liter) food-grade cooking pouch, and vacuum seal.
- Immerse the pouch in the water oven and cook for at least 1 to 1-1/2 hours.

- Remove the pouch from the water oven and the chicken from the pouch. Pat the exterior of the chicken dry with paper towels.

- In a skillet, over high heat, melt the butter and quickly sear the chicken on both sides for color.

- Deglaze the pan with the tequila and scrape up the flavorful brown bits. (For safety, remove the skillet from the heat when adding the tequila to stop flare up.)

- Move the chicken to a warm plate and drizzle with the tequila pan sauce.

- Squeeze on the lime juice and dress up with chopped chives. Enjoy!

CHAPTER FORTY SEVEN
SOUS VIDE CHICKEN WITH ENGLISH MUSTARD AND BROAD BEANS

Ingredients

- 6 chicken thighs, skin on and bone in
- 6 find slices of lemon
- 350g shelled broad beans
- 1 golden onion, finely diced
- 1 tbsp English mustard
- 2 tbsp butter
- 2 tbsp plain flour
- 400mls white wine
- 300mls light chicken or vegetable stock
- 100mls single cream
- Extra virgin olive oil
- Olive oil
- Unsalted butter
- Vegetable oil

- Sea salt
- Black pepper

How to prepare

- Preheat the bath to 66.6°C.

- Season your chicken thighs on both sides with salt and pepper and put them into your vac pouch, then drizzle the lemon slices in extra virgin olive oil and place one on each chicken thigh (non skin side) inside the pouch, then vac seal.

- Put into the water bath for 90 minutes, and when done, remove and chill down until cold inside the pouch and set aside pending when you need them.

- When you're ready to eat, fry the onion in a little olive oil on a medium heat until translucent, then add the knob of butter and when melted, add the flour. Using a whisk mix the flour into the butter, then add the mustard, wine and stock and whisk in until the roux is mixed and begins to thicken, this will take a few minutes. Turn onto a low simmer and stir periodically.

- Take the chicken out of the vac pouch and carefully remove all the meat juices and lemon slices and put them into the mustard sauce, then pat the chicken skin dry with paper towel and season with salt and pepper.

- In a frying pan put a large knob of butter and glug of vegetable oil, and turn onto a high heat. When the butter foams and begins to brown, add the chicken thighs skin side down and do not move once in the pan.

- Cook on the skin side down for 4 to 5 minutes, then season the bare side of the chicken and turn over for another 4 to 5 minutes, while this is happening, add the shelled broad beans and single cream to the mustard sauce to heat through.

- Serve the chicken on top of the mustard sauce with warm baguette and a large glass of vino.

CHAPTER FORTY EIGHT
SOUS VIDE MACKEREL

Mackerel is well-suited to pickling since it has a strong flavor and, as a result, it is not overpowered by the vinegar in the pickle. Pickling food sous vide has a number of advantages over traditional methods. It needs fewer liquid and the food absorbs the flavor of the pickle more rapidly.

Ingredients

- 70ml of white wine vinegar
- 30ml of water
- 30g of sugar
- 3g of salt
- 4 mackerel fillets, pin boned

How to prepare

- Mix the white wine vinegar and the water, and then add the sugar and salt. Stir until totally dissolved.
- Gently lay the mackerel fillets inside a vacuum bag without overlapping them. Add the pickle to the bag and seal.
- Put in the fridge for 30 minutes.
- Once chilled, take the fish out of the bag and gently dry them with kitchen paper.

CHAPTER FORTY NINE
SOUS VIDE SEA BASS

With its firm, nearly meaty flesh and its subtle flavor, sea bass has long been a favorite of many skilled chefs and home cooks. Cooking sous vide is good way to make this popular fish since the use of a sealed vacuum bag locks in moisture and stops drying out.

Ingredients

- 2 sea bass portions, each weighing 120g
- dash of olive oil
- pinch of sea salt
- Preheat the water bath to a temperature of 50^0C.

How to prepare

- Sprinkle the sea salt over the sea bass and seal in a vacuum bag with the olive oil.
- Put the bag in the water bath and leave it to cook for 15 minutes. This cooking time is for quite thick portions of sea bass; lessen the time slightly if using thinner pieces.
- Gently slide the cooked fish out the vacuum and pat all over with kitchen paper to dry.
- Lie the fish skin-side down in a very hot frying pan. Sear over a high heat until the skin is crisp and golden then serve immediately

CHAPTER FIFTY
SOUS VIDE BEEF AND PRUNE TAGINE

Ingredients

- 1kg beef shin, cut into cubes
- 2 onions, finely chopped
- 1 pinch of saffron, ground to a powder
- 1 tsp ground ginger
- 1 tsp ground cinnamon
- 1 tsp garlic powder
- 250g of prunes, stoned
- 1 tbsp of runny honey
- 50g of unsalted butter, chilled
- 5 ice cubes
- 1 tbsp of olive oil
- salt
- pepper

SOUS VIDE COOKBOOK

How to prepare

- Preheat a water bath to 75°C

- Richly season the diced beef. Heat the oil in a large frying pan and sear the beef in batches, for a couple of minutes, or until it is browned all over. Move the seared meat to a large dish and set it aside

- Decrease the heat under the pan, add the onions and stir occasionally over a low-medium heat for about 10 minutes, or until soft and golden – add a little more oil if needed. Remove the pan from the heat

- Tip away any meat juices that have collected in the dish that the beef has been resting in, or it will be sucked out during vacuum sealing

- Add the onions, saffron, ginger, cinnamon, garlic, prunes and some salt and pepper to the beef and toss thoroughly to evenly distribute the aromatics

- Transfer the meat into a vacuum bag and add the honey, butter and ice cubes

- Vacuum seal the bag and put in the preheated water bath for 12–16 hours

- 10 minutes before you are ready to serve, place the couscous in a bowl and mix through a good pinch of fine sea salt. Add the extra virgin olive oil and add 450ml of hot water from the kettle. Cover up and leave to stand while you dress up the tagine

- Snip the bag open and pour the beef into a large, warmed bowl. Flip through half the toasted almonds and scatter the remaining half over the top, along with the sesame seeds and coriander

- Fluff the couscous with a fork and serve it with the tagine

CHAPTER FIFTY ONE
SPICED PINEAPPLE WITH WHIPPED CREAM CHEESE YOGHURT AND GINGER BISCUITS

This sous vide cooked dessert tastes awesome. Perfect for a family meal or get together.

Ingredients

- 1 x pineapple
- 1 tsp Chinese five spice
- 2 tsp lemon zest
- 1 tsp crushed pink peppercorns
- ¼ tsp nutmeg
- ¼ tsp cinnamon
- 1 tsp allspice
- 200mls white wine
- 100g soft dark brown sugar

Whipped Cream Cheese Yoghurt

- 250 g cream cheese
- 100g natural yoghurt

- 1 ½ tbsp. Vanilla yoghurt
- Grated star anise
- 100g crushed ginger nut biscuits

How to prepare

Spiced pineapple

- Peel the pineapple
- Mix all other ingredients together, place everything under vacuum. Seal and cook sous vide at 85c for 12 hours

Whipped Cream Cheese Yoghurt

- Beat all the ingredients together until it is smooth and silky, set in the fridge overnight
- Build the dish and top with the crushed ginger biscuits

www.ingramcontent.com/pod-product-compliance
Lightning Source LLC
Chambersburg PA
CBHW052143110526
44591CB00012B/1840